LIFE

JO[illegible] CASH

With his Gibson in 1958.

JOHN HAMILTON

LIFE

Johnny Cash
An American Legend

EDITORIAL DIRECTOR Kostya Kennedy
DIRECTOR OF PHOTOGRAPHY Christina Lieberman
EDITOR Robert Sullivan
CREATIVE DIRECTOR Anke Stohlmann
WRITER-REPORTERS Michelle DuPré, Amy Lennard Goehner, Daniel S. Levy
COPY CHIEF Parlan McGaw
COPY EDITOR Barbara Gogan
PHOTO EDITOR (2018 UPDATE) Rachel Hatch
PHOTO ASSOCIATE Sarah Cates
PHOTO ASSISTANT (2018 UPDATE) Steph Durante
PRODUCTION Richard Shaffer
SPECIAL THANKS Rosanne Cash, John Carter Cash, Danny Kahn, Lou Robin, Tom Tierney, Ché Williams

TIME INC. BOOKS, A DIVISION OF MEREDITH CORPORATION
SENIOR VICE PRESIDENT, FINANCE Anthony Palumbo
VICE PRESIDENT, MARKETING Jeremy Biloon
EXECUTIVE DIRECTOR, MARKETING SERVICES Carol Pittard
DIRECTOR, BRAND MARKETING Jean Kennedy
SALES DIRECTOR Christi Crowley
ASSOCIATE DIRECTOR, BRAND MARKETING Bryan Christian
ASSOCIATE DIRECTOR, FINANCE Jill Earyes
ASSISTANT GENERAL COUNSEL Andrew Goldberg
SENIOR MANAGER, FINANCE Ashley Petrasovic
SENIOR BRAND MANAGER Katherine Barnet
ASSOCIATE PROJECT AND PRODUCTION MANAGER Anna Riego Muñiz

EDITORIAL DIRECTOR Kostya Kennedy
CREATIVE DIRECTOR Gary Stewart
DIRECTOR OF PHOTOGRAPHY Christina Lieberman
EDITORIAL OPERATIONS DIRECTOR Jamie Roth Major
MANAGER, EDITORIAL OPERATIONS Gina Scauzillo

SPECIAL THANKS Brad Beatson, Brett Finkelstein, Melissa Frankenberry, Kristina Jutzi, Seniqua Koger, Kate Roncinske

Published by LIFE Books, an imprint of Time Inc. Books,
225 Liberty Street • New York, NY 10281

Vol. 18, No. 17 • August 31, 2018

We welcome your comments and suggestions about LIFE Books. Please write to us at:
LIFE Books, Attention: Book Editors
P.O. Box 62310, Tampa, FL 33662-2310

FRONT COVER Performing on Danish television in 1971.
JAN PERSSON/REDFERNS/GETTY
BACK COVER MICHAEL ROUGIER/LIFE/THE PICTURE COLLECTION
THESE PAGES At the Newport Folk Festival in July 1964.
DAVID GAHR/PREMIUM/GETTY

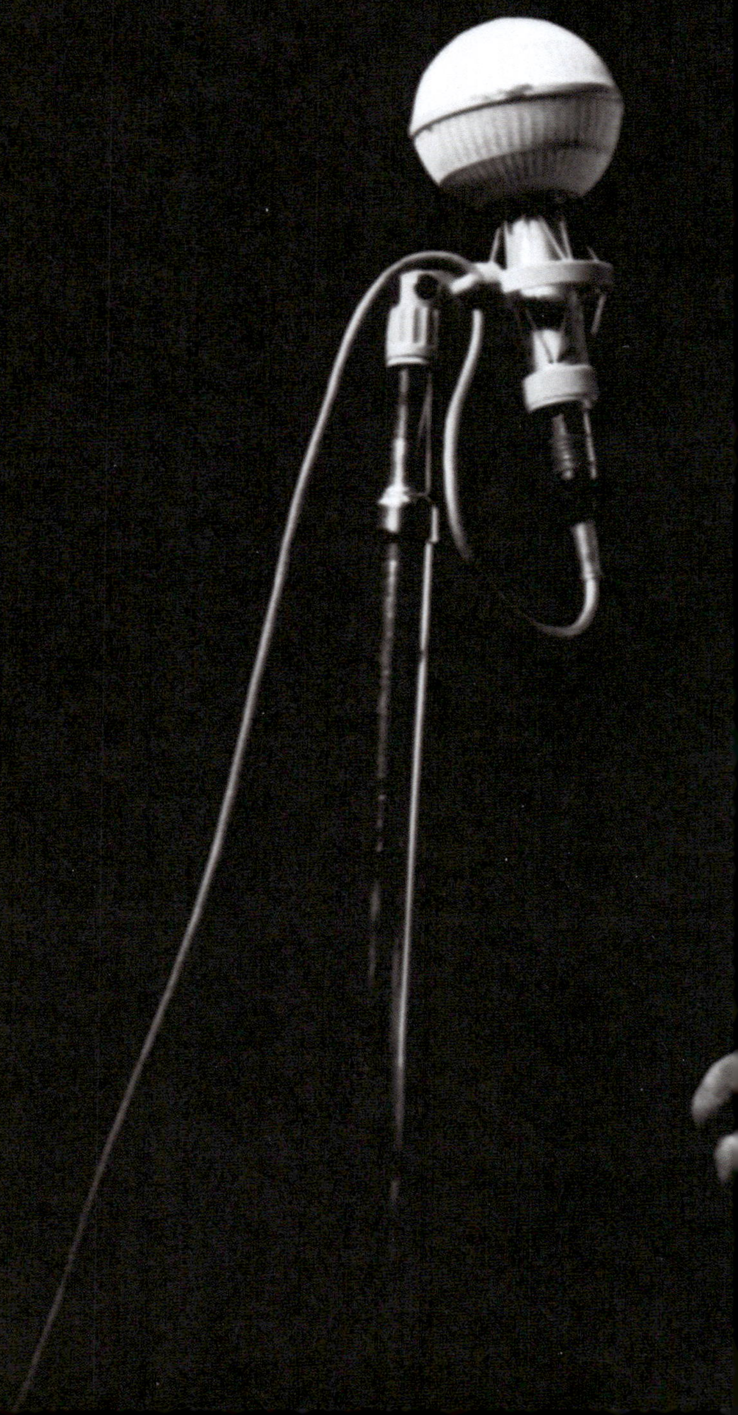

4 Looking at Family Photos with Rosanne Cash

8 John—Before "Johnny"

14 From Memphis to Nashville

34 A King of Country

48 The House on the Lake

62 The Prison Concerts

72 The Man in Black

88 The Legend Lives On

LOOKING AT FAMILY PHOTOS WITH

ROSANNE CASH

Johnny Cash's first child, with Vivian Liberto Cash, was Rosanne, born in 1955 in Memphis, right around when Johnny was recording his first tracks there for Sun Records. Both Johnny and June Carter Cash, Rosanne's stepmother, died in 2003, and Vivian died in 2005. Rosanne is the one still with us who was there for most all of what you will see in the pages to follow.

For more than three and a half decades Rosanne has been in the highest echelon of American singer-songwriters, and in recent years has won acclaim for her fiction and nonfiction writing as well. On her last three terrific albums, *Black Cadillac, The List* and *The River & the Thread*—leading up to 2018's *She Remembers Everything*—she has revisited her family's legacy. Who better, then, to travel through these photographs? Rosanne lives in New York City, and on a Saturday morning in the spring of 2013, she shared her thoughts after poring over these pages.

"I looked through all of the photographs and they're really wonderful," she begins. "I thought that there were some surprising choices, things that were really unexpected." She isn't entirely familiar with the earliest material from the collection out at Arkansas State: "My grandmother and grandfather on the porch, and the photos of my dad in the Air Force: It's really comprehensive, and I was really happy to see those included. And once he started singing professionally, the pictures of fans. One picture I really love is the one of him and Luther [Perkins] and this huge crowd of people in the background. That's fantastic."

Perkins was Johnny Cash's guitarist from the very beginning—1954—until Perkins's death in 1968; the picture Rosanne refers to is on pages 24 and 25, and was taken as stardom was first happening for her father. The photograph kindles other memories: "Luther and Marshall [Grant, the bassist in the Memphis act that evolved into "Johnny Cash"] were always around. Marshall was always a lot closer to my family because Marshall's wife and my mom were best friends. But Luther was always around, too, and his wife—and it was devastating for everyone when Luther died. The band was always there, they were always there. It was absolutely like family."

Rosanne talks warmly about Marshall Grant. "I loved Marshall. I looked at [the picture on pages 72–73] and thought about them all meeting. My dad's brother Roy worked at the Chrysler dealership, and Luther and Marshall were mechanics, and Roy came in and said, 'My brother's coming back from the Air Force and he could meet you. He plays guitar.' And my dad walks into the bay where they were working and Marshall looks up and the hair on his back stands up when he sees my dad. He knew that the rest of his life was bound up with this man."

There are pictures of other friends and collaborators, from later in the career. "Kris and Willie and Waylon," Rosanne says with a smile. "Dad was really, really close to Waylon and Kris particularly. Willie was a friend, but Waylon and Dad were always over at each other's house. Waylon—he was a sweetheart. He had his demons, but he was a sweetheart. And Kris: They were brothers, they were soul brothers. I feel right now that Kris is the closest link I have to my dad.

"I'd seen a lot of these photographs, but the ones that I hadn't seen before were really moving to me. They weren't just kind of stock Johnny Cash pictures, but showed some side of him, some depth, that hadn't really been captured before.

GOLBE/ZUMA

IN THE LATER 1960s, Rosanne is at the far left, along with her sisters, Kathy, Tara and Cindy. At the far right is her grandmother Carrie. This photo was snapped in an age when folks couldn't just say, "Grandma, you had your eyes closed!" and then take a second picture with their phone.

And of course I really liked some ironic things, fun things, like him in those black-and-white loafers, and he's holding his Gibson, his Johnny Cash Gibson, and he's in the pale blue socks. It's just such an awesome picture—some kind of cross between rockabilly and jazz and the Kingston Trio."

It is suggested to Rosanne that her dad's music was relatively catholic through the years—hard to pigeon-hole as stone-cold "country." She says, "Absolutely. He was ecumenical, very much so. We liked that. He took my brother [half brother John Carter Cash, John and June's son] to Metallica. He took me to see Strawberry Alarm Clock when I was 15 years old. Talk about ecumenical! Totally ecumenical."

"Where did you go to see Strawberry Alarm Clock?" she is asked.

"It was in Hendersonville, at the Hendersonville High School. I remember liking them, and I remember visiting my dad for the summer and there was a really small crowd, and I and my dad sat in the front row."

"Did the band know who he was?"

"Oh, hell yes."

"Did they have more than one song?"

She laughs and says, "Not really, no. Everybody knew 'Incense and Peppermints' and that was about it. But Dad enjoyed himself I think."

"He probably couldn't go anywhere in Hendersonville—or Tennessee—where they didn't

EDMOND TERAKOPIAN/PA/GETTY

ROSANNE has successful careers in singing and writing. Her 2014 album, *The River & the Thread,* won three Grammy Awards, including for Best Americana Album, and revisits the singer's roots. "The album is an exploration of both the geography, the characters and my ancestral connection to the South," she says.

know who he was, right? Was he the center of it when you went out as a family, or did he try to fade into the background?"

"No, no," Rosanne answers quickly, "He was the center, he was the center. He would decide on hot summer afternoons that we were going to the movies, and we would go from theater to theater. I was 11 or 12, or early teens or late teens even, and we would go to four movies in a day. Or he would decide that we were going roller-skating and he would rent the roller-skating rink."

"It's good being Johnny Cash!"

"Well, he was so famous he couldn't go anywhere and have his peace, so if he wanted to go anywhere with his kids and enjoy himself, he had to do those things."

"What about those summer photos at the lake house?" Rosanne is asked. "It looks like a magical time for a kid. In the movie [*Walk the Line*] they showed the lake house accurately, but here you people really are . . ."

"Well," she says. "A movie's a movie. The photos are real. But I remember it as almost unreal. It was idyllic for a kid in the summers. I can't tell you how great it was, everything about it. It was a perfect life, those summers—the pool and the boat and the southern cooks every afternoon at 4:30, and it was just the people who came in and out and my dad at the height of his health and power and orchestrating all of these great things for the kids to do, taking us to the farm or . . . The jeep riding was huge. Every day in the summer, there was a jeep ride."

Noted to Rosanne: "There's a photo of him with John Carter on his lap helping him drive [pages 58–59] and he looks so happy."

"Yeah, he was, he was—it was probably the happiest time of his life. And those are some of the best memories of my life."

"We have a lot of pictures of family reunions. What were those like?"

"The family gatherings?" She laughs again. "What were they like? Well, it depended if everyone was clean and sober. Some of them were great. In the late 1970s and early '80s, they were fantastic. But other times, some people would come in not the best shape, and that would blow things up.

She turns to another subject: "It's wonderful, too, looking at the pictures of my mother. There's the one of her getting on the plane and she's clearly pregnant [page 27]. I'm not sure who she's pregnant with, though. There's also this photo where my mom and dad are at a dinner table talking to someone. It's Mitch Miller [page 29], and my mother—the look she had on her face. I remember my parents talking about him. And the look on my mom's face, where she's just not buying what he has to say. Like he wants them to do something that she's not buying. She was like that."

That's the other side of these pictures, of course: the professional side of Johnny Cash the singer, not John Cash the father and husband. Rosanne indicates that in her family, which of course evolved into the even larger Carter-Cash clan, the two often overlapped. "At the lake house, or anywhere, there was always music, always music. When you couldn't say anything else, there was always music."

"Do you remember the legendary 'guitar pulls' in the lakeside room?"

"Yeah, I remember them—always in the lakeside room, as it was called." Memories of the big rooms at the lake house open a door into all that family history, she says.

"Did you sing?'

"Yeah, I did, when I was starting to become a songwriter. And I still cringe to think of myself singing for some of those groups of people, with those songs I wrote. It was the hubris of youth. I don't know, I was 18 or 19, and the audience, well, I remember Billy Graham being there once, and I remember Tammy Wynette and George Jones and Roy Orbison and Mickey Newbury . . ."

"Those were kind people in your jury."

"Yes, yeah. Very kind people. It was hard for me to wrap my mind around it. I was really young, like 18, and learning how to play guitar and write songs. My dad was so encouraging. He would take me on stage with him and tell me that even the worst stuff I wrote was wonderful. He was the ultimate support. And as I got older and got a recording contract—which, by the way, he was instrumental in me getting, which I didn't learn until much later—I started pulling away a bit. I wanted to do it on my own, you know, and I wanted to work this out on my own, without people constantly referencing him in my work. He understood that, too. I think it may have hurt him a bit, but he understood it totally. And we got through that, the thing everyone goes through in their twenties, and then everything was just great. We would talk about music and politics every time we got together. We talked about music and politics all the time—and books . . . and books. Music and politics and books."

"It must have been nice," it is suggested, "to see him have that late-in-life renaissance as a singer."

"Renaissance?" Rosanne answers. "He had a lot of renaissances. That was one of the key character traits of my dad: He was like a phoenix. He would go down really dark and deep and come back. He did that so many times in his life. And after the last few years when he was so sick, the music really kept him alive, and it was his final burst—his final burst of genius. And some geniuses do that, you know, they don't let it crush them, the addiction or the illness or the whatever, and . . .

"I saw him a lot, a lot, in those last years," she continues. "It was good. The family today? Well, Tara, my younger sister, she's out in Portland and has two sons, and we're as close as any sisters can be. Our boys love each other like brothers. My other two sisters and half brother: We're close like any adults are. Rosie, June's daughter, is dead, as you know. It's hard, the passage of time. I'm still close to Etta Grant, Marshall's wife.

"The house [by the lake] is gone, as you know. The cabin's still there. John Carter still lives in Hendersonville, and he keeps up the recording cabin, and he records there. But that's it: the cabin, and their graves. They're buried there, and it's heartbreaking.

"The lake house, I think about it now, and it's like a dream and a myth. I wrote about the fires once. It's so weird. Roy Orbison's house was the next house down the road, and it burned down. And ours. And . . .

"Well, there certainly are a lot of memories." ■

JOHN BEFORE "JOHNNY"

YES, HE WAS JOHN before Johnny, and in fact he was "J.R." before John, as we will shortly learn. Here is the future legend at 11 years of age in 1942. At this point the family had already moved from Kingsland, Arkansas, to Dyess, and J.R. is already a six-year veteran of singing alongside his parents and siblings (he had six brothers and sisters in all) while working in the cotton fields.

EVERETT

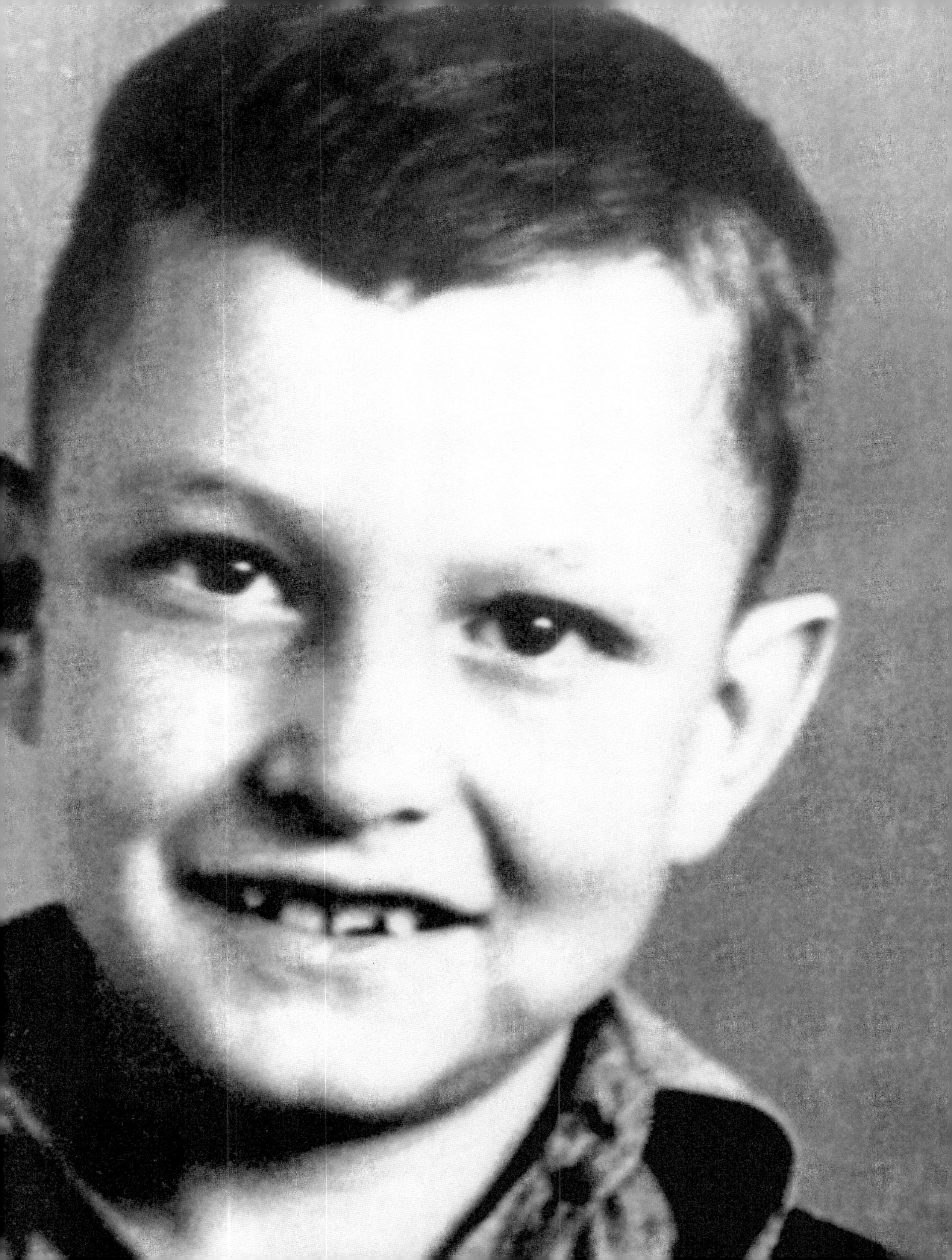

ON THE PORCH of the house in Dyess circa 1943, this is *most* of the Cash clan. But where's J.R.? Well, taking the photo. In Arkansas, everyone knew him as J.R. That's how he knew himself—in fact, it was his real name. His parents, Ray (in the hat) and Carrie (far left), couldn't think of a suitable name for the fourth of their eventual seven children, and so they called him J.R. Working in the cotton fields of Dyess from the age of five, the boy answered only to calls of J.R. Meanwhile, he soaked up the Depression-era travails of his family and friends. Clearly, he filed these away, for later they would emerge in his songs. The family farm was flooded more than once, and "Johnny" Cash would sing of this in "Five Feet High and Rising."

J.R. was greatly affected by the death of his older brother Jack in a 1944 table-saw accident. Both boys and Carrie had a foreboding that morning, and she urged Jack to skip work cutting wood and go fishing with J.R. But Jack knew the family needed the money, and he reported for duty. Johnny Cash wrote much later that he looked forward to meeting his brother in the afterlife, and he commemorated Jack throughout his life. When he enlisted in the U.S. Air Force in 1950, he was told that initials alone would not do—he needed a proper name. He chose "John R. Cash," and if he felt this brought him yet closer to his late brother, that's exactly the kind of spiritual connection that would always be important to this man, a seeker all his days. In any event, this would now be Johnny Cash's "real name"; the world would know him by his stage name, Johnny, but he would always be called John by his friends and later family members (the Arkansas folks still called him J.R.). As for that family, from oldest to youngest the kids were Roy, Louise, Jack, J.R., Reba, Joanne and Tommy. This youngest would also be a successful country music artist and, now in his seventies, continues to sing—carrying on, with Rosanne, John Carter Cash and others, the family legacy.

CASH FAMILY COLLECTION, ARKANSAS STATE UNIVERSITY

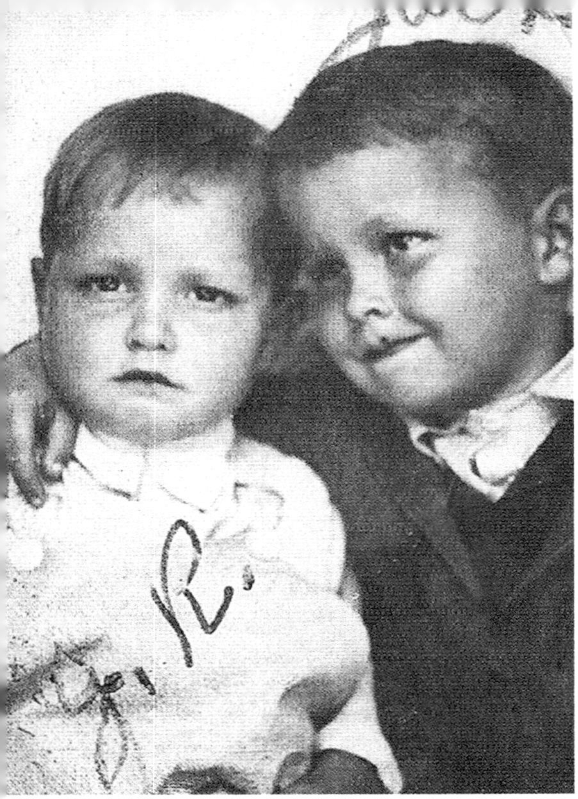

J.R. AND JACK, seen at left when J.R. is still a toddler circa 1936, are close as brothers and as boyhood friends, and would be linked eternally by tragedy. Below: The Cash family in Dyess in 1949, from left: Roy, Carrie, Louise, Tommy, Ray, Reba, Joanne and J.R. Opposite: Joanne, J.R. and Tommy. Both of these Cash boys did stints in the service: J.R., changing his name to John, in the Air Force and Tommy in the Army, after which, already a veteran of a high school band, he played some with Hank Williams Jr. Tommy's biggest hit, in 1969, would be "Six White Horses," a song dedicated to the two assassinated Kennedy brothers and to Martin Luther King Jr.

CASH FAMILY COLLECTION, ARKANSAS STATE UNIVERSITY (3)

FROM MEMPHIS TO NASHVILLE

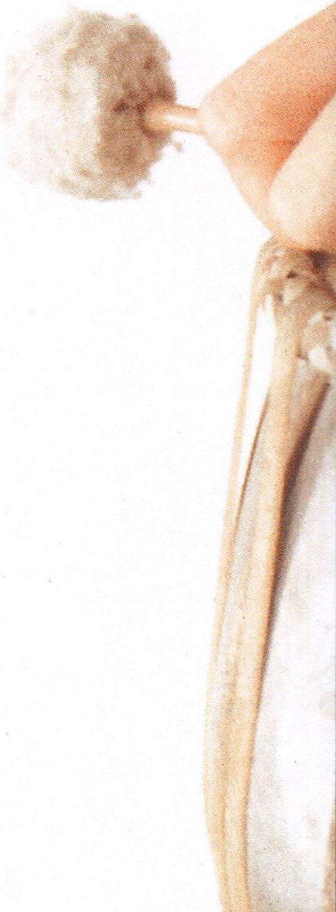

WE NOW ENTER a great stash of photography from the archives of Sony Music Entertainment, which in 1988 acquired Columbia Records, John's home base for the bulk of his career. Some of these photographs are bizarre and some of them John might have wished destroyed before his death. Would this be Exhibit A? Possibly—but there's more fun stuff ahead. The outtakes of publicity shoots, when the record companies were trying to figure out precisely how to position an artist—playing with whether this guy or that gal might be "crossover"—are always irresistible. Johnny was certainly going to be a rockabilly or country performer, but here he looks like he was auditioning for Tito Puente's band.

CRPS

THIS FAMOUS PHOTOGRAPH is the opposite of a rarity in that it has been seen a thousand times—but then again it is something of a rarity because you have these four very famous guys, and there aren't even four pictures of them together to commemorate what happened that December day in Memphis. So it needs to be presented in a book such as ours: as a signpost, as a crucial episode in the story that was now becoming the Johnny Cash saga.

How had he come to this point in time, where he was included that afternoon in what would later be called the Million Dollar Quartet? The same way he had become "Johnny"—through the auspices of legendary producer Sam Phillips.

One day in Memphis, John had taken a deep breath and gone down to the Sun Records studio from which he and (from left in the photo) Jerry Lee Lewis, Carl Perkins and Elvis Presley would emerge as stars. "I went and knocked on that door and was turned away," he later remembered in a story he told in slightly different ways at different times. "I called back for an interview three or four times, was turned away. So one morning I found out what time the man [Phillips] went to work. I went down with my guitar and sat on his steps until he got there. And when he got there I introduced myself . . . Evidently, he woke up on the right side of the bed that morning. He said, 'Come on in. Let's listen.'" Phillips wasn't taken with Cash's gospel stuff, but said, "Come back tomorrow and bring some musicians." When John returned with his Tennessee Two mates Perkins and Grant and some rockabilly material, including "Hey Porter" and later "Cry, Cry, Cry," Phillips came fully around. When he was pressing these first records in 1955, the producer said to himself and to his latest protégé that the name "Johnny" was catchier than "John." And that was that.

The next year—on December 4, 1956, to cite the historical date—Elvis dropped by Sun during a Carl Perkins recording session; Jerry Lee Lewis was playing piano. Cash was also there, and when the four of them started fooling around with gospel tunes, Phillips left the tapes running. Those sessions are today immortal, with "Down by the Riverside" perhaps the highlight. Unfortunately, our man John didn't sing on that number.

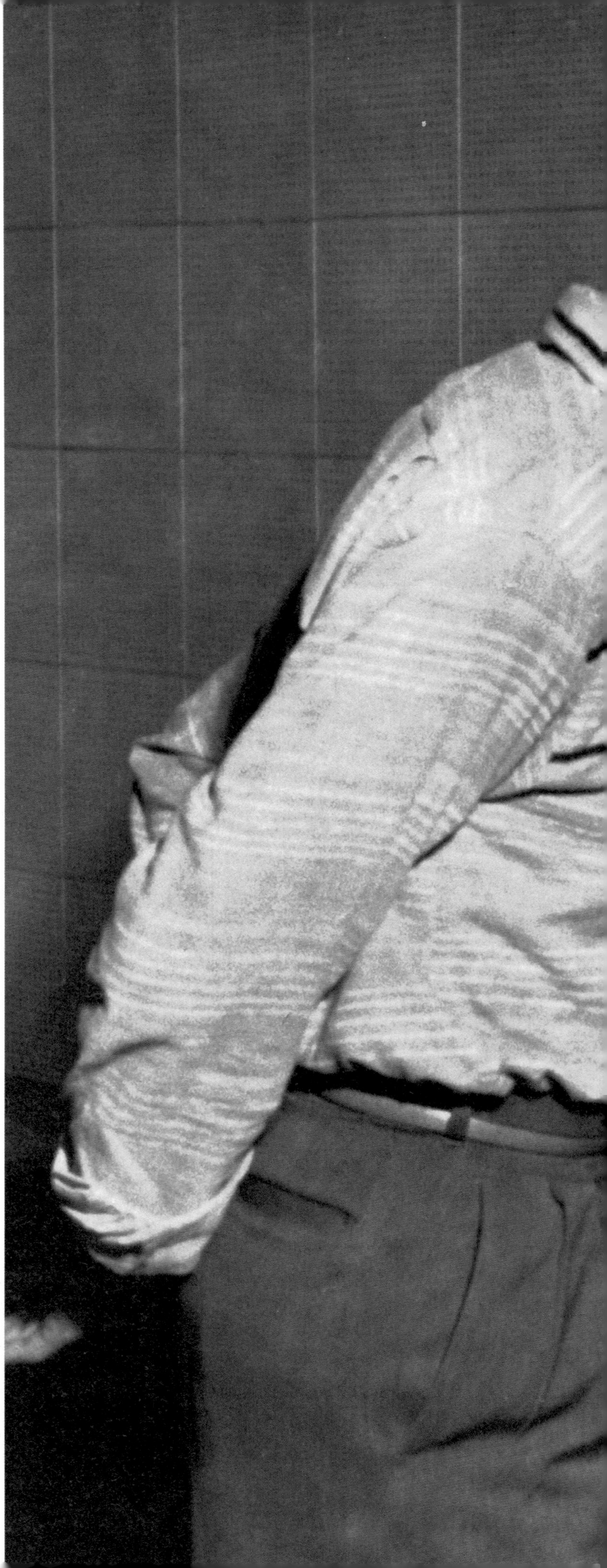

MICHAEL OCHS ARCHIVES/GETTY

GUY GILLETTE (3)

THE GIGS GOT BETTER. Cash's third release on Sun, the 1956 single "I Walk the Line" (which was meant for Vivian) backed with "Get Rhythm," established him as a rising star. His first performance with the Tennessee Two, seemingly only moments before, had been in a church basement playing for elderly ladies. Now he was being booked into the biggest halls in Memphis and was taking his act on the road—the Louisiana Hayride, the Grand Ole Opry, even (on these pages) a television show that traveled far beyond Tennessee.

IT'S NOT ALWAYS EASY or altogether honest to put together a showbiz career. As we see on the following two pages, when the cameras are sent in by the handlers to chronicle the life of a star, that star must pose, feign casualness, suggest a certain faux intimacy. If there are other women besides the wife, if there are very late nights fueled by booze and drugs, if those late nights are becoming a problem—all of this must go unsaid, and certainly unseen. (Just by the way, though: John Carter Cash tells LIFE that booze was never the problem; drugs were. "Dad had very little problem with alcohol," he says. "His thing was the pills.") In the tumultuous dozen years of the marriage of John and Vivian Cash, there certainly was joy—they had four daughters: Rosanne, Kathy, Cindy and Tara—and John became a star. But meantime he developed those drug addictions and generally carried on. These were states of affairs that couldn't be hidden from Vivian.

The color portrait here from 1958 is, as Rosanne Cash has said, a standout. How about those two-tone shoes!

DON HUNSTEIN

Johnny Cash

JOHN HAMILTON (3)

Johnny

JOHN HAMILTON

THE COUNTRY of country music was also, in the late 1950s and early '60s (and still proudly today) the country of such things as stock car racing and big-time college football, and before too very long Johnny Cash could fill a stadium as readily as Fireball Roberts or 'Bama versus Auburn. Here he's alongside Luther Perkins in 1958, and this is precisely the kind of "who cares?" photo that got buried more than a half century ago but that speaks volumes—and is a lot of fun to look at—today. In 1958, Johnny, knowing he was hot (as that year ended, he was the third-highest-selling country artist in America, and was appearing nationwide, prime time, on such programs as *The Jackie Gleason Show*), followed Elvis's lead and left the comforting confines of Sun Records and its nurturing paterfamilias Sam Phillips to sign a big-money deal with Columbia Records, where he would remain for much of his career (just as Elvis would stick with RCA). Many boardroom negotiations later, Columbia is today part of Sony—and that's why this precious legacy of photography is available to us all in this book.

AIRLINES
KXLA
POPULARITY AWARD
Johnny Cash
The most popular recording artist
of 1958 as selected by the
listeners of KXLA
the Western music station,
Pasadena

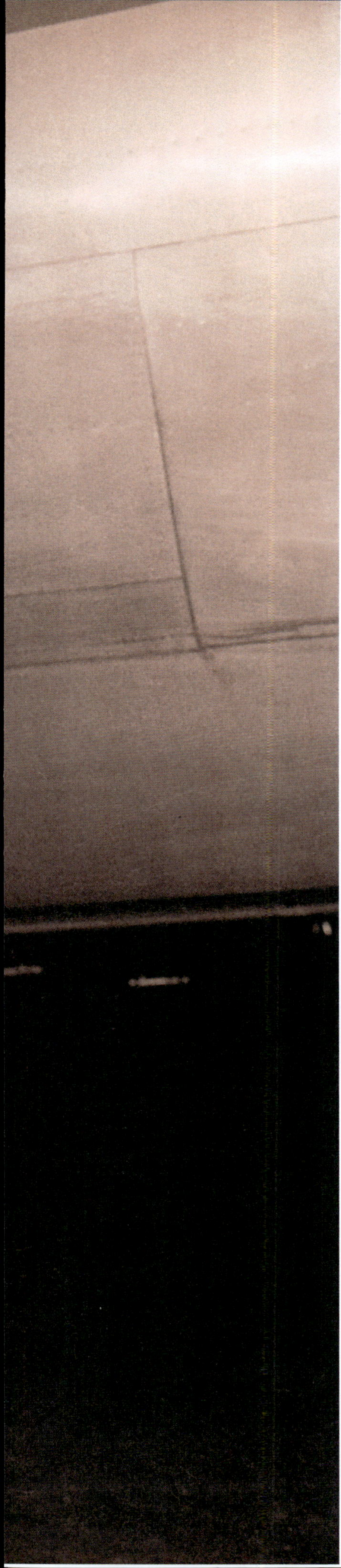

JOHN HAMILTON (2)

IN A MORE INNOCENT AGE a popularity award from one of many country music radio stations was something to show off. (Today, if it's not a CMA trophy or a Grammy, forget it.) Above: En route from one gig to another are John and Vivian, certainly happy to be booked on a major airline. In that era, when rock 'n' roll or country artists had become big enough to be in demand nationwide, they quite often had to start puddle-jumping by plane—any plane. Buddy Holly, Ritchie Valens and Jiles Perry "J.P." Richardson Jr. (better known as the Big Bopper) were killed on the "day the music died" in 1959, and country's queen, Patsy Cline, died in Tennessee in 1963, when the Piper she was traveling in went down. In the first of those two famous crashes, Waylon Jennings, who was playing bass in Buddy Holly's Crickets, gave up his seat on the plane to the Big Bopper—and was thus spared. He and Johnny Cash were already friends, and would become better ones, eventually collaborating in the Highwaymen. We'll see Waylon later in these pages.

THERE'S NO MISTAKING Johnny Cash, whether it's the husky-dusky voice, the bluesy beats, the boom-chicka-boom rhythm on the up-tempo numbers or, visually, the dangerous mien, the hue of the clothing (yikes! here we have . . . white!) or the guitar riding up to his chin. Here and on the next two pages: The man at work once he had become a star. Above is a business session with Mitch Miller, then an A&R man for Columbia, with Vivian sitting in. On the pages following these, we will discuss Johnny in the studio for Columbia during the hit-making days—and elsewhere, afterward—in a bit more depth.

DON HUNSTEIN (2)

IN THE STUDIO, whatever studio that might be in whichever period of his long career, Johnny was a consummate pro and at ease. His friend Willie Nelson legendarily recorded his masterpiece *Red Headed Stranger* in a day and a half, and has said that most of his recordings were made on a first or second take—third at the most. Johnny wasn't quite that carefree, but he too came prepared, and always checked his ego at the door. "I don't know if he was aware of the magnitude of his presence, but pretty much anybody who came into contact with him was intimidated by him, for the most part," said Rick Rubin, who years later produced Johnny's acclaimed last sessions, the so-called American Recordings. "But he was just such a humble person, in a few lines of casual conversation he was able to make everyone feel okay. Again, I don't know how much of that was preplanned, or done on purpose, but I saw it happen a lot. It may have just been a natural urge to put people at ease; it may not have had anything to do with celebrity. But it definitely worked, in terms of just taking the intimidation factor down, and making people feel comfortable." Even in the days when heavy drug abuse was the ruin of many a public

DON HUNSTEIN (3)

performance, Johnny could still pull it together in the studio, as we see here in pictures made in 1959. He always focused intently on the lyric, said Rubin—he knew exactly what he was trying to convey when he sang each song, even if the message was based on the suggestion of someone else. It has often been said that you can hear this on the American Recordings, but really: You can hear it on all of them. There's a remarkable double-disc called ***Personal File,*** a collection of 49 songs his family stumbled upon after Cash's death: recordings he had made by himself, alone with his guitar, in his home studio. "There were a lot of songs that I wrote when I first started out in my musical career that I never recorded for one reason or another, either I didn't feel good about them . . . or maybe the record company didn't feel like they were up to par or something," Cash said into the microphone about these remarkable songs that no one knew he was about to record. "But some of those songs must have had something, because I still remember them. And every once in a while, when I'm driving along in the car, I sing them over and over to myself." He finally sang them for posterity, and we are all the luckier for it.

APPEARANCES can deceive, and they do to a degree in this family portrait inside the Cashes' new home in Los Angeles. This looks like a happy family—the very happiest. Vivian and John are trying hard to insulate the children from their troubles; they are sometimes successful. "We were rich in love, but dirt poor," Vivian later wrote, looking back to the earliest days of their relationship. "We woke up every day never knowing where our next dollar would come from. We just struggled together, blissfully unconcerned about the future." Johnny was the one who brought the problems on, of course, and we've already alluded to that in these pages. Suffice to say: After the $50,000 bonus from Columbia Records in 1958 and then the overtures from the movie studios, they moved to Southern California with their three daughters (Rosanne, Kathy and Cindy; and soon after, a fourth, Tara, was born, in 1961). The house seen here was in Encino—bought from Johnny Carson, no less—and later there would be a ranch. Vivian sensed a "dangerous current" after the move to California, but this can translate prosaically into drugs and life on the road. The good news: The children grew up healthy, and as happy as could be.

DON HUNSTEIN

JOHN WAS by this point known to the whole world as Johnny—introducing himself nightly with "Hello. I'm Johnny Cash," a simple line that, in the 1960s and '70s, became the country equivalent of "Ladies and gentlemen, the Rolling Stones." He was on top of the world, even as he was bottoming out. In this next period, he would find salvation of a sort, thanks to June and God, while learning only too well that demons are tough to shake and hard to keep at bay.

DON HUNSTEIN

A KING OF COUNTRY

DON HUNSTEIN

IT'S FUNNY: Back in the day, stars used to allow photographers into their homes; they are far more wary, far more encased, and do much less of this today. And yet magazine and record-album editors and designers seemed to prefer the elaborately staged portraits or, if they did choose shots from the "home shoot," obvious set-ups with Dad or Mom goofing with the kids. So many of the real gems went unseen, or perhaps wound up in the artist's family albums. This photograph is from 1960, at his home in California. Throughout life, John spent many of his best hours just like this (as the *Personal File* discs prove): communing with his guitar, his songs, his thoughts, his worries—and whomever else he might summon.

SAM PHILLIPS MAY HAVE WANTED ROCKABILLY from Johnny Cash rather than the gospel songs that John brought with him to that first audition at Sun Records, but the artist himself would never forgo the music he had been raised on. Most of the *Personal File* recordings are gospel or gospel-tinged, and, like Elvis, Willie Nelson and George Jones, John dedicated whole albums to nothing but spirituals: *Hymns by Johnny Cash, Hymns from the Heart* (seen here, outtakes from the 1961 photo sessions), *A Believer Sings the Truth, The Gospel Road, The Holy Land.* For this last referenced LP, John traveled to the place in question—Jerusalem and elsewhere in the Middle East—for inspiration and photo opportunities. His fans realize as well that much of his late-in-life American Recordings albums, even before the *Unearthed* box set, comprised either gospel songs written by himself or others (his friend Kris Kristofferson's "Why Me Lord") or rock songs reimagined with neo-gospel settings (U2's "One," Nine Inch Nails' "Hurt").

DON HUNSTEIN

IN THE EARLY and mid-'60s, the nighttime was the wrong time for John, and the nightlife was the bad life: That's when he got in trouble. In 1965 alone he was busted in El Paso for trying to smuggle amphetamines from Mexico in his guitar case, and then he got himself banned from the Grand Ole Opry after he strafed the footlights with the microphone stand, shattering glass and causing wonderment and fright. In 1966, Vivian would file for divorce. His retreat, as much as he had one, was to spend the days at home in his new house in Hendersonville, Tennessee, or in the studio (left, working on the German-language version of "I Walk the Line"). John was deeply experienced at this point and knew how to man the mixing board. But he also kept it simple and did things as he always had. In fact, Luther Perkins and Marshall Grant were still on guitar and bass in his recording band as well as on the road, just as they had been at the start. The "boom-chicka-boom" sound remained in place.

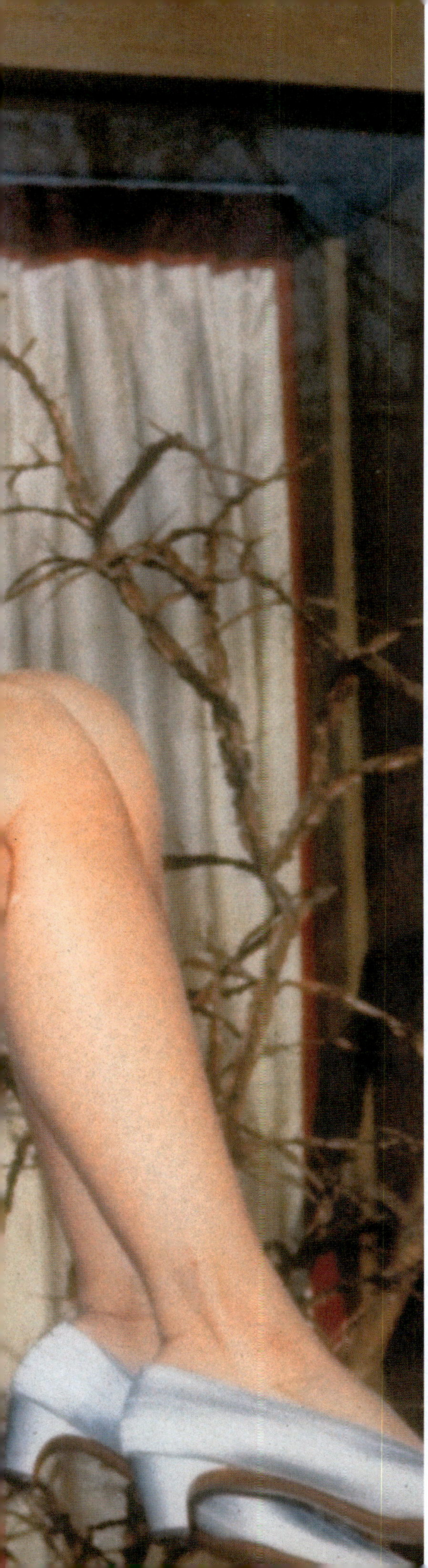

COURTESY HOUSE OF CASH

JUNE AND JOHN had a big success together in 1967 with "Jackson," which went to No. 2 on the country charts and was a popular crossover song as well. Early the next year, they were on the road in Canada, and on one particular night the gig was at a place called the Treasure Island Gardens in the city of London, Ontario. John hemmed, hawed, then popped the question onstage in front of some 7,000 or so fans, and he and June were married on March 1, 1968, in Franklin, Kentucky—as we see here. They would be husband and wife for 35 years, until her death in 2003 of complications following heart-valve surgery, quickly followed by his of respiratory complications of diabetes (and complications of a life of bad living, plus complications of a few months on planet Earth without June). That marked the end of the saga of Johnny and June.

John was happy when he hoisted his bride in '68, and happiness indeed prevailed in the early years of the marriage. June helped John cope with his addictions, and he kicked some of them for a goodly while. With June's counsel, John embraced fundamentalist Christianity, a strain of God-worship he had sung about over and over through the years—the years when he was recording professionally and the earlier years when he was harmonizing on spirituals in the fields or in church. This was a major turning point for Cash in 1968—for John the man more than Johnny the entertainer. A turning point or, perhaps, a large red STOP sign. Either way, it was the perfect thing at the time, and he was very happy. So was June.

John's generosity as a performer—and as a star—was made manifest again, even in his relationship with his wife. Although June, as a member of the Carter Family, was folk music royalty, there was no question who had the bigger career as a solo artist, and who should be the family's principal breadwinner, but at every step of the way John made sure that June was by his side—onstage as well as at home. They shared the Grammy Award for Best Country & Western Performance Duet, Trio or Group for their 1967 recording of "Jackson," and tore it up with that song on a nightly basis. Their first album together was somewhat provocatively titled *Carryin' On with Johnny Cash & June Carter,* and there were more in the 1970s: *Johnny Cash and His Woman* and *Johnny & June.* When John was in the studio solo, June was back home, thoroughly running the show. Upon June's death years later, Rosanne Cash said in a eulogy at the funeral, "If being a wife were a corporation, June would have been a CEO. It was her most treasured role."

COURTESY CASH FAMILY

AS MIGHT BE EXPECTED, John, once he had cleaned up, was a better father as well as a better husband and a better companion generally. As mentioned earlier, he and Vivian had four lovely daughters, seen here with Dad (from left: Rosanne, Tara, Cindy and Kathy). June's own two daughters were Rebecca Carlene (who would become the country singer Carlene Carter) and Rosie (who would also become a singer before her accidental death at age 45 by carbon monoxide poisoning, which occurred in 2003: a terrible year for the Carter-Cash clan, which lost June and John at the same time). As the girls graduated from high school, those who chose to do so segued into the family act. Rosanne worked in wardrobe during her dad's tours, then became a backup singer and finally took the occasional solo; Rosie sang backup on her stepfather's TV show. There would be another singing Carter-Cash to join this brood, and we will meet him on the pages immediately following.

A SON JOINS six daughters on March 3, 1970, when John Carter Cash, John and June's only child together, is born in Nashville. John Carter, as he is known to all who know him, will grow to be a musician, singer-songwriter, producer (he has been involved with numerous Grammy-winning albums), writer, skilled outdoorsman and carrier of the family flame. He first worked as a producer on his mom's CD *Press On* in 1999, then assisted Rick Rubin on two of his dad's American Recordings albums. He produced his mother's *Wildwood Flower,* which won the Grammy for Best Traditional Folk album in 2003, and in 2005 he earned three nominations for *Unbroken Circle: The Musical Heritage of the Carter Family.* Meantime, he wrote children's books and also, in 2007, a memoir: *Anchored in Love: An Intimate Portrait of June Carter Cash.* In the pages ahead, we will revisit some of what John Carter wrote about in that book, but for now suffice it to say: It was difficult to recount a sometimes wonderful, sometimes harrowing upbringing. His parents loved one another unconditionally, John Carter has said and written, but there were fights, there was the hovering fear of divorce (at least, as sensed by their children), and there was the constant specter of addiction, which eventually visited June as well as John. In 1970, however—with a healthy baby boy and Johnny Cash as big a star as ever, with his television show a major hit—everything was coming up roses.

J.T. PHILLIPS

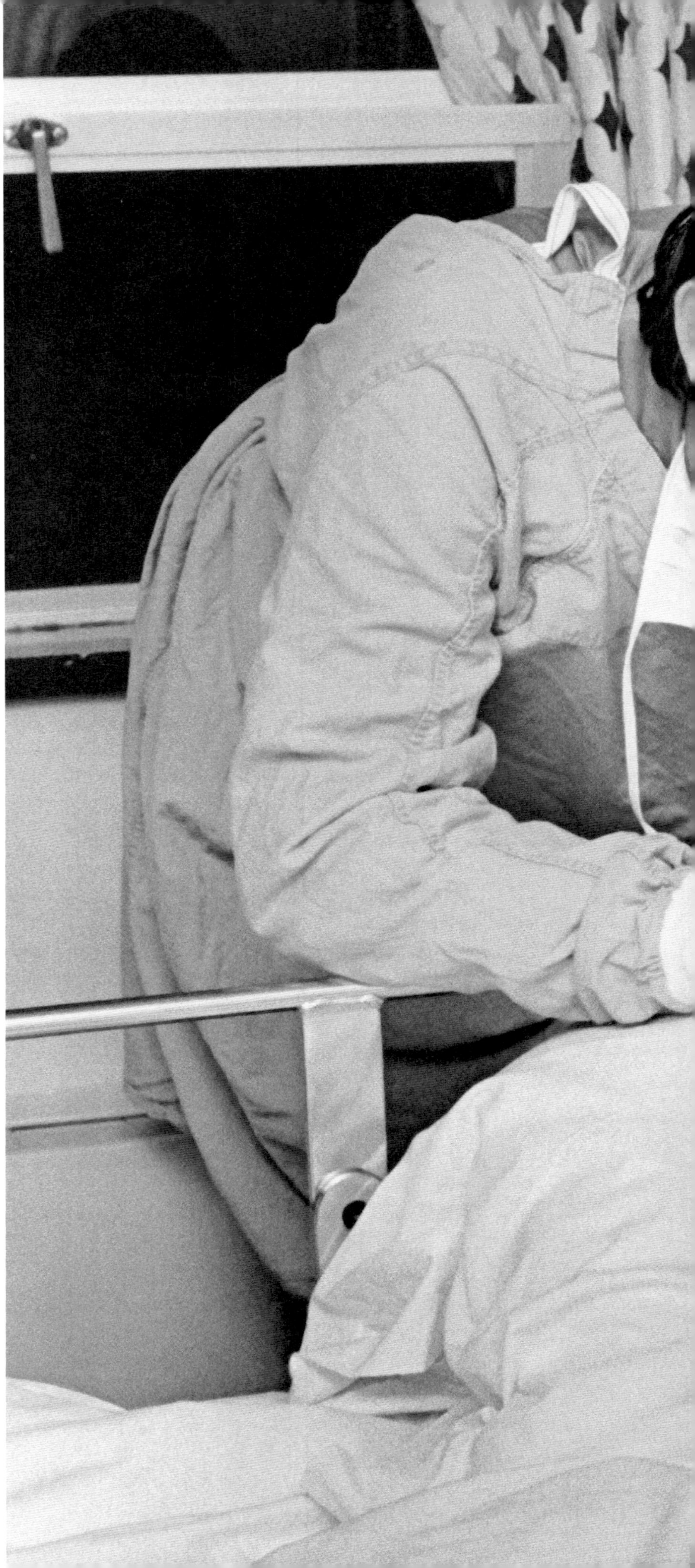

BOB CATO

THE HOUSE ON THE LAKE

"WELL, I MISS the sounds of Tennessee," Rosanne Cash wrote and sang, in a song she composed after her father died in 2003, "and the smell of heavy rain / The roses in the garden / Laugh before the pain/ But I hear his voice close in my ear / I see her smile and wave / I blink and while my eyes are closed / They both have gone away." In the chorus: "Blue bare room, the wood and nails / There's nothing left to take / But love and years are not for sale / In our old house on the lake . . ."

BOB CATO

THE HOUSE HAD A PROSAIC address—200 Caudill Drive in Hendersonville, Tennessee—but a poetic aspect in its beautiful expanse, its rough-hewn situation and all the human drama enacted there through the years. It wasn't so much on Caudill Drive as it was on Old Hickory Lake, and after California and New York it was the place John came home to, to live with June and all sorts of children and eventually grandchildren. It was the home that J.R. Cash had always sought and always, after the flood of fame, needed. The motto on the Cash family coat of arms reads "Better Times Will Come," and in John's way of thinking: That could have been the motto of the lake house.

It is obvious to its fans that we haven't yet mentioned *Walk the Line,* the fine biographical film—we haven't played off it, said where it might have been right, where it was a little bit wrong. That has been purposeful; John's life was very much more complicated than those two hours could capture. Nor could any narrative we might write do justice in 96 pages. So we have decided to let these pictures speak largely for themselves. That said, anyone who has seen the film and now looks at the photographs on the next several pages must remark: The movie sure got that right. It did. As deft as the performances were—June and John (shortly before they died) approved Reese Witherspoon and Joaquin Phoenix as the leads—the film was even more faithful to the lake house in Hendersonville and rightly suggested how much that property meant to John. The house itself was featured in the film, and some of its rooms, circa the period in question, were painstakingly recreated in constructed sets.

John bought the house in the late '60s, not realizing that he was on the verge of a second wave of superstardom, this one thanks to that great American nation-mover-and-shaker, television. When *The Johnny Cash Show,* broadcast from down the road at the Ryman Auditorium (Hendersonville is 18 miles northeast of downtown Nashville), caught on with a national audience, the lake house became not only a retreat from fame but, as we shall see, something of a clubhouse for John's latest generation of pals.

© JIM MARSHALL PHOTOGRAPHY LLC

JOHN WOULD OWN OTHER places, even unto Jamaica, but Hendersonville was where he could relax. With its natural setting, near where Roy Orbison had a place, this was quite a spread, stretching along the rocky shoreline of Old Hickory Lake. Outdoors, there was a swimming pool and a bell garden, but the charm of the woodland near the water was an attraction best left unspoiled. The house itself was a rustic mansion: a 13,880-square-foot rambling edifice built on a solid rock foundation. A highlight consisted of a number of immense 35-foot-diameter rooms, and there were seven bedrooms and five full bathrooms. The house was filled with hand-carved dark wood furniture that the Cashes found during their global travels—John and June were both big shoppers and prone to the extravagant gesture, which sometimes caused financial problems—and the walls featured portraits of family members and close friends such as Waylon Jennings and Carl Perkins. One table supported a collection of acoustic instruments once played by the original Carter Family. There were also framed gold records, of course, but the one for "I Walk the Line" was hung at a smaller ranch house across the street at 185 Caudill Drive, and therein lies another story. This was called Mama Cash's House, and indeed was where John's mother lived in her last years. (She pitched in by working at the House of Cash museum in Hendersonville, downtown in the building where the family's business affairs were also centered.) John, too, lived his very last days at the ranch house, when getting around the lake house in his wheelchair proved problematical.

BOB CATO

BOB CATO

HAPPINESS was more easily attained in Hendersonville than elsewhere, and certainly, as we see here, John and June are happy at the lake house. It should be added: According to John Carter Cash's 2007 book on his mother, happiness was more general in the 1970s than the '80s, when a slump in his father's career caused financial difficulties and his parents were forced to sell jewelry and other possessions to pay their sizable domestic staff. But earlier, when John's variety show was going strong, the lake house was the center of a rolling party, and June, who ran the place, was the perfect hostess. Eventually, John and some of his musical friends would make their way through a hallway and down some stairs to the lakeside room where they would engage in their legendary "guitar pulls." John remembered to LIFE in 1994: "In 1968, '69, when I was doing my TV show, we'd invite singers and guitar players over for dinner. Afterward, everyone had to take the hot seat and do at least two songs. The most memorable night was in '69. Kris Kristofferson sang 'Me and Bobby McGee,' Bob Dylan sang 'Lay Lady Lay,' Joni Mitchell sang 'Both Sides Now,' Graham Nash sang 'Marrakesh Express,' and Shel Silverstein sang 'A Boy Named Sue'—all in the same night. People had never heard those songs, and the very next week, when I played San Quentin prison, I took 'A Boy Named Sue' with me."

UP

J.T. PHILLIPS (3)

FOR A YOUNG BOY, the lake house was heaven, and surely life in Hendersonville nurtured John Carter's love of the outdoors. "The house was large, but it was home, and never felt stuffy or empty," he tells LIFE. Here he plays with the dog and is attended (above) by nurse Winifred Kelly, and visits with Grandma and Grandpa Cash and their bird (top). In his memoir, John Carter said that as he grew older he became aware of tensions in his parents' marriage, and, later still, of their addictions—John relapsing in the 1980s and '90s, June becoming reliant on prescription drugs.

JOHN CARTER, seen here helping Daddy drive on the property, remembered that when he was a child, he cried as he heard his parents fight for hours one day. He wrote that the arguments between the two never became physical, but that he heard his mother threaten to leave the family. He lived in fear that his parents would divorce. That particular day must have been the worst, because he remembered it best: The parents argued and argued, and eventually became aware that their boy must have been a witness. Finally, they called to John Carter and said they had to deliver some news. He held his breath, expecting to hear that the family was coming apart. Instead, they told him they had decided to renew their marriage vows—which they did do. In promoting his book, which was published four years after his parents' deaths, John Carter said they would have wanted him to write it, because they always chose to be honest about life—the good and the bad. John Carter now looks back, 15 years after his parents' deaths, and sums up: "My mother and father had a love like none other. Though there were rough times, the strength of their relationship endured. When my mother and father came together, onstage or off, something special happened. My mother had a way of softening the Man in Black. Somehow he was more tender by her side. Gentler." The ballad of John and June was a true country song, more real than any lyric.

J.T. PHILLIPS

MICHAEL ROUGIER/LIFE/THE PICTURE COLLECTION

WHENEVER THERE WAS a guitar handy, music might fill any room in the lake house—and there was always a guitar handy. Here, Roy Orbison takes his turn on the hot seat before an intimate audience that includes (from left) Johnny; Braxton Dixon, who built the lake house, and his wife, Anna; Kris Kristofferson, with two women close by; June, in the shadows; and Jack Palance. After both June and John died, four months apart, the lake house was sold by John Carter to the British singer Barry Gibb and his wife. The former Bee Gees star said he intended to renovate, but he promised to keep the house true to its heritage and preserve it as a place of homage to Johnny Cash. As they were planning the remodeling in 2007, the house caught fire and burned to its foundations. Famous neighbors gathered, many of whom had close connections to John, June and the house itself. "So many prominent things and prominent people in American history took place in that house," said the singer Marty Stuart, who lived right next door and had been married to John's daughter Cindy in the 1980s. "Everyone from Billy Graham to Bob Dylan went into that house." He added that for John, the house had been "a sanctuary and a fortress." Said another Caudill Drive neighbor, Richard Sterban of the Oak Ridge Boys, a group that had been helped at regular intervals by John: "Maybe it's the good Lord's way to make sure that it was only Johnny's house."

AS A JAILBIRD, John was a fly-by-night visitor, never in for the long haul. He had the reputation of being an hombre toughened by hard experience in stir, but this is legend, not fact. He was never in state or federal prison except to sing songs, and he spent a grand total of seven nights in jail for various offenses through the years. The most violence he encountered in custody was probably when, after being arrested for public drunkenness in Starkville, Mississippi, he broke his toe by kicking the bars of his cell. But as for playing to prisoners and lifting their spirits: Well, he was the Bob Hope of the behind-bars circuit. Here, he and June arrive at Folsom on January 13, 1968.

THE PRISON CONCERTS

16

FOLSOM PRISON, where John grabs a smoke before his performance for the convicts in 1968, and San Quentin were the two famous prison concerts, but that's entirely because they were recorded. There were many others, some much earlier than the well-known late-'60s shows.

For reasons probably linked to his personal sense of empathy, John was always drawn to prisoners. He first became aware of Folsom State Prison in Sacramento County, California, when he was in the Air Force and, in 1953, was shown a documentary film, *Inside the Walls of Folsom Prison*. Cash was moved to write "Folsom Prison Blues," and that became the A-side of his second single for Sun Records. Inmates heard it, took to it, and some of them started corresponding with the singer. The bolder of them asked if he might perform at their institutions, and in 1957, Cash sang at the state penitentiary in Huntsville, Texas. News spread on the inmate grapevine that the show, filled with songs of trial and hardship as well as fun novelty numbers, had been terrific. "The word got around among the convicts that I was one of them, because of the songs I sang," John told LIFE. "So I started getting a lot of requests for prison concerts and started doing a lot of them. I first did San Quentin prison [in California's Marin County] in, I think, 1958. Merle Haggard can tell you the date. He was in the audience."

(Haggard was authentically hardened in a way Cash was not: Busted for attempted robbery in 1957, he spent two years and nine months in San Quentin, where he ran a gambling and bootlegging operation out of his cell. He later said that the Johnny Cash concert inspired him to join the prison band, and of course the rest of that is history—and a different book.)

John went on from San Quentin to many other prison shows through the years, and by 1967 he realized that these concerts might be worth capturing on record. He pitched the idea, and Columbia execs took it to officials at San Quentin and Folsom. The folks at Folsom quickly said yes, and on January 13, 1968, the tapes rolled.

WELCOME
JOHNNY CASH

JUNE WASN'T TENSE but was properly sober-minded at the prison, as was everybody. Yet once the concert began (after two days of rehearsals and an inspiring visit by California governor Ronald Reagan), the bandmates and inmates all had a ball—as can be seen here. The first show was slated for 9:40 a.m. and the second for 12:40 p.m. on January 13, and the program included Carl Perkins singing "Blue Suede Shoes," the Statler Brothers doing "Flowers on the Wall" and Cash performing, among other selections, prison songs such as "The Wall" and (of course) "Folsom Prison Blues," plus yuck-it-up numbers like "Dirty Old Egg-Sucking Dog." A highlight of the concert was a song written by Glen Sherley, an inmate, and that story will be told on the next pages.

© JIM MARSHALL PHOTOGRAPHY LLC

JOHN PRAYS in the prison chapel during downtime. His thoughts are surely with the inmates, and perhaps he focuses on Glen Sherley—the subject of one of the most fascinating stories in Johnny Cash lore. Incarcerated for armed robbery, Sherley was also a man of musical talent. He had written and sung a song and had given it to the Reverend Floyd Gressett, a Ventura priest who regularly visited Folsom. John picked up the story from there when talking with LIFE: "The night before I was going to record at Folsom prison, I got to the motel and a preacher friend of mine brought me a tape of a song called 'Greystone Chapel.' He said a convict had written it about the chapel at Folsom. I listened to it one time and I said, 'I've got to do this in the show tomorrow.' So I stayed up and learned it, and the next day the preacher had him in the front row. I announced, 'This song was written by Glen Sherley.' It was a terrible, terrible thing to point him out among all those cons, but I didn't think about that then. Everybody just had a fit, screaming and carrying on. After a year or so, he was paroled. He did an album, a good one, and he wrote 'Portrait of My Woman,' which Eddy Arnold had a hit record off of. [What happened to Sherley], there are two stories, and I don't know enough to tell you which one to believe. It was either suicide or cancer—I know there was a gun involved. The last time I saw him, he was back in California, working for some big cattle company, feeding 10,000 cattle a day. He lived in the cab of a semi truck. He didn't want any more of public life. Just couldn't handle it." For the record: Glen Sherley died in California on May 11, 1978, from a self-inflicted gunshot wound to the head.

© JIM MARSHALL PHOTOGRAPHY LLC

THIS SAN QUENTIN photograph, chosen for every good reason for the Columbia album cover, is another of our signature pictures that, even in a book of rarities, is a required inclusion. Any volume aspiring to tell the Johnny Cash story needs the Million Dollar Quartet moment, and needs this strong image from 1969. It captures the singer about to reemerge, big-time, in the spotlight. His TV show is on the horizon and now there's this album; in the coming months they will combine to push each other to higher heights. As for Cash's prison concerts: They were hardly over. He not only continued to perform before inmates, he became even more of an activist for prison reform. On July 26, 1972, he was introduced by Tennessee senator William Brock to the U.S. Senate Subcommittee addressing the issue, and told them that inmates needed, almost above all else, a modicum of hope. Less than three months later, John gave his first free jailhouse concert outside the U.S., at Österåker Prison just north of Stockholm, Sweden. So here's a trivia answer: The concert was recorded, and *Johnny Cash på Österåker* is not only John's third great prison-concert LP, but—if you can find it in vinyl—a true rarity among rarities.

THE MAN IN BLACK

J.T. PHILLIPS

JOHNNY CASH WAS STILL a stranger to a substantial part of the American audience as late as the summer of 1969—it's a fact. He had had the country hits, but that didn't do it for certain segments of our postwar society. Some folks revered him as a god, some folks didn't know him from Adam. That was about to change because he was about to turn around melodramatically, look the TV camera square in the eye and sonorously intone, for the ten thousandth time and for the edification of those he was meeting for the first time ever, "Hello. I'm Johnny Cash."

NO SMOKING

J.T. PHILLIPS

NOTHING ELSE has the capacity to bolster—even cement—a celebrity's public image in the American mind-set like exposure on national television. We perhaps had heard those yeah-yeah Beatles sounds on the radio in early 1964, but then we saw them on *The Ed Sullivan Show* and, wow, that was something else. We knew Michael Jackson had grown up some and was no longer the cute little kid singing with his brothers, but then he moonwalked before our eyes on the Motown 25th Anniversary special, and the next morning at the water cooler there was nothing else to be discussed. Madonna was arguably a child of MTV as much as of radio.

Johnny Cash had been playing with the black-clothes thing for a while; if you flip through the pages of this book you see him growing darker year by year, and by the time he's appearing for the cons and the cameras at Folsom and San Quentin he's got the look locked and loaded. His sound had been set in stone for a while, and was formidable. It's worthwhile to pause here and note: It wasn't a strictly country sound. It wasn't the least bit twangy or high lonesome—beautiful sounds, to be sure, but off-putting to some northern ears. It was bottomless in its bass and altogether different. He sang folk songs as often as he sang country songs, and when he went up-tempo it was always rockabilly, which is to say rock 'n' roll. In his autobiography, Cash, he wrote that if he were stranded on a desert island, the recordings he would need would include *The Freewheelin' Bob Dylan,* Merle Travis's *Down Home,* a compilation of Jimmie Davis's greatest gospel hits, Emmylou Harris's *Roses in the Snow,* Rosanne Cash's *The Wheel,* any gospel collection by Sister Rosetta Tharpe, "something by Beethoven" and a selection of *You Are There* radio broadcasts. There you have it!

So one Saturday night after dinner in the summer of '69, America turns the dial—there were no remotes back then, children—and America sees there's an off-season replacement show for *The Hollywood Palace,* its beloved variety hour. Suddenly this severe-looking oily-haired man is staring at them, and even though he's saying "Hello," he seems a bit menacing. Then he starts to sing, which has always had a way of mesmerizing folks. And then he proceeds to unwrap one of the strangest, most wonderful, most ecumenical American entertainment packages ever to grace the small screen. *The Johnny Cash Show* would only last a few seasons and, despite how fondly it is remembered, and despite the fact that in the who-wants-to-watch-TV? days of summer it reached No. 1 once or twice, it wasn't really a reliable Top 10 show (17th for the complete 1970 season). But it was vastly influential because it reached across all sorts of fences in the severely picketed America of 1969 and '70, and offered to shake a hand. The guest lists and set lists—as well as the pictures—that will be reviewed on the next several pages are scarcely to be believed, even all these years later. John left a number of great legacies, personal and professional. This was one, and it cut both ways. It was professional, but even more: It was personal.

J.T. PHILLIPS (7)

TO KEEP THE PEACE with the network and with many thousands of viewers, John welcomed such performers as Bob Hope (middle row, right), Burl Ives and Peggy Lee to the stage, but also Linda Ronstadt, Kris Kristofferson, Neil Young, Gordon Lightfoot and James Taylor. Merle Haggard and Tammy Wynette were guests, of course, and so were the Cowsills and the Monkees—of course. In the gallery above, clockwise from bottom left, we see Brenda Lee, O.C. Smith, Ricky Nelson, Mama Cass Elliot, Hope and the Everly Brothers. And on the opposite page are two iconic American folksingers: Judy Collins (top) and, on the very first program, Bob Dylan. For those who liked it, this was the greatest show on earth.

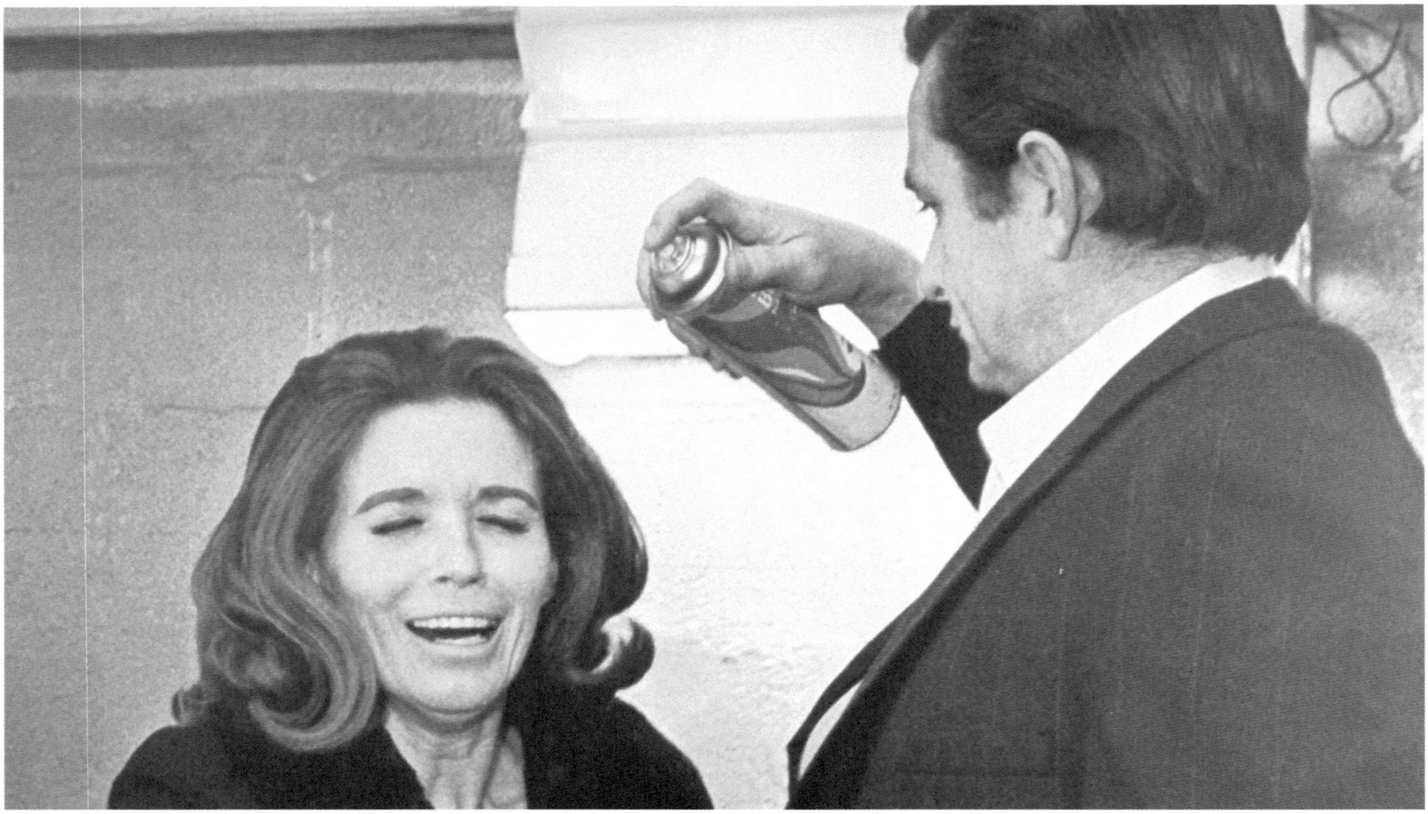

J.T. PHILLIPS (4)

A CONSTANT STAR on John's show, and now the guiding star in his life, was June, seen here, goofing and performing with her husband. They dueted for the TV audience on not only "Jackson" but also such numbers as "Turn Around" and "'Cause I Love You." June reprised her earliest hit, a No. 9 country single in 1949. Any guesses? It was a rendition of the Christmas-season chestnut "Baby, It's Cold Outside," which is often done sexy but not when it's being sung by one of the wholesomer-than-thou Carter Family girls alongside the country/comic duo Homer and Jethro. June's devoutness influenced John; the new Johnny Cash, a proud Christian, wouldn't shy from his faith on the air, despite the skittishness of ABC execs. Then again, he adamantly refused their suggestion that he cut the word stoned from his performance of Kris Kristofferson's "Sunday Mornin' Comin' Down." So maybe he was ecumenical after all—or just a stubborn cuss whenever the suits tried to tell him what to do.

J.T. PHILLIPS (3)

FOR THE FINALE of *The Johnny Cash Show*'s second season in 1970, John was onstage with a mature woman and started to tell a story in that from-the-pulpit way of his. He reminisced about the first song he had ever sung in public, "when I was 12 years old, back at a little church in Dyess, Arkansas." The song was "The Unclouded Day," and he planned to do this hymn again on this night, for the folks watching at home. "And here's the lady that accompanied me on that song, my mother." Carrie and the son she had named J.R. 38 years earlier then performed beautifully and simply. John gave his mother a kiss and said, "Momma, that was fine." The year after he died, a collection of gospel songs by John, all of which had been taught to him by Carrie, was released under the accurate title *My Mother's Hymn Book*. He had recorded those 15 songs when old and frail, and he said in the liner notes that this was the favorite of all of his many, many albums.

J.T. PHILLIPS

AGAIN, CARRIE is at the keyboard and again it is 1970: Here and on the next four pages, a gathering of the Cash clan for Ray and Carrie's 50th wedding anniversary celebration. In this picture, John's father, Ray, is looking on from the end of the piano, and several of John's siblings surround. Sister Louise, now Mrs. Joe Garrett is at near left, and then there's sister Reba (Mrs. Don Hancock) and brother Roy. On either side of Ray are sister Joanne (then Mrs. Billy Ingle; now Joanne Cash Yates) and brother Tommy, and then John himself. On the following page, clockwise from top: Grandkids Kelly Hancock, Jeff Ingle, Mark Cash and Tara Cash steal the show; then the middle generation gathers, with Joanne, Louise, Reba (in front) and Tommy, John and Roy; and finally, in a mix of those two generations, John holds John Carter Cash as John's eldest daughter, Rosanne, looks on happily. On the page after that, the celebrants cut the cake. These folks have come a long way from Dyess to a fantastic lakeside spread in Tennessee, but they're still the same people.

J.T. PHILLIPS (4)

J.T. PHILLIPS

IN THE CENTER is the happy couple after a half century of marriage: Ray and Carrie Cash. Behind them are, from left, Gloria Cash, Carlene Smith (known as the country singer Carlene Carter), Reba Hancock, Louise Garrett, Roy Cash, Tommy Cash, Joanne Ingle, John and John Carter Cash, Rosanne Cash, Kathy Cash and Ricky Hancock, Don and Reba's son. The kids in front are, from left, back row: Rhonda Ingle (Joanne's daughter), Mark Cash (Tommy's son) and Jeff Ingle (Joanne's son). Second row, from left: Paula Cash (Tommy's daughter), Tara Cash (Johnny's daughter), Charlotte Ingle (Joanne's daughter), Cindy Cash (Johnny's daughter), Timmy Hancock (Reba's son) and Paul Brent Garrett (Louise's son). Lastly, the three young ladies in the front row, from left: Darla Cash (Roy's daughter), Kelly Hancock (Reba's daughter) and Rosie Nix (June's daughter). Certainly much of the conversation during this celebratory gathering is about Carrie and Ray and the progress of—and burgeoning of—the Cash family. Certainly, too, a lot of it is about the glory John has conferred on the clan through the years: a big singing star, and now a major TV star, too. Everyone in this photo is, at the moment, riding high.

IN THIS LAST CHAPTER, John takes a look back, and at one point in the past, LIFE prompted him, asking the question: "What singers do you particularly admire?" We weren't looking for "Trent Reznor" or "Bono," but in any event John answered, "Hank Snow is my favorite. I just bought his boxed set last month. I was with Rick Rubin, my new producer. We went to Tower Records, and I saw it and said, 'Did you ever listen to Hank Snow?' And he said, 'No, I don't think I've ever heard of him.' I said, 'Well, you're going to.' I bought it, we took it to his house, and Rick kept it." This was John's last campaign: listening to what he wanted to, telling the world why it was great, singing and playing a lot of it, and preparing for the future.

THE LEGEND LIVES ON

BRIAN LANKER

WAYLON JENNINGS, WILLIE NELSON, Kris Kristofferson, and Johnny represented, for some fans, the greatest generation of postwar country music singers, songwriters and stars. Whether they were coming together as the Highwaymen in the mid-'80s to the mid-'90s, or cracking up as John and Willie are doing at top while trying to smile politely, they'd earned the fancy backdrop and the kind lighting. There was no hiding the wrinkles at this point, or the wars waged through the years. But—almost weirdly—these four were back on top, in advance of Garth Brooks, Travis Tritt and all who would follow. "You know," John told LIFE late in this period, "I miss the tried-and-true and the dyed-in-the-wool. I guess that's a typical comment from an artist my age. Glory for the new artists, great. But country radio doesn't program hardly anybody over 40. Country music is about tradition. And they're losing that tradition, in my mind, anyway."

JIM MCGUIRE (3)

ANDY EARL (2)

THE WORD "RENAISSANCE" is overused in the press. It is trotted out to describe a moderately successful comeback single or movie, or someone getting back to work after rehab. But there is, or can be or should be, a spiritual connotation to the word, and certainly before he died John enjoyed what was called—everywhere, by everyone—his final renaissance. He told LIFE how he came in touch with Rick Rubin, the producer who believed in him: "He heard I wanted to cut ties with Mercury Records because it had been an unsuccessful venture, on their part and my part. So Rick called my manager and said he'd like to sign me. He didn't say he'd like to talk about it, he said he'd like to sign me. So when we met, I asked him, 'What kind of album would you like me to record?' And he said, 'Whatever Johnny Cash is, that's what I want on a record.' He made me feel like Sam Phillips made me feel." Yes, indeed: Some of life's journeys were coming around again. Many of the songs were old songs, and some of the new ones that John would come to own were done in new ways, which were old ways at heart. There would be four—or IV—American Recordings released while John was alive, II more posthumously, plus the box set *Unearthed.* The pictures on this page are outtakes from the photo sessions for his first Rick Rubin–produced album, *American Recordings.* The concept was merely conceptual—John wasn't throwing away the guitar or walking away from the music, not quite yet.

JOHN'S LAST ALBUM while he was alive was *American IV: The Man Comes Around;* the portrait here in the field and the one at the end of our book were made for the *Unchained* CD. He was in great pain during his final years; to return to the testimony of Rosanne Cash that began our book: "He was so sick [and] the music really kept him alive—his final burst of genius." Perhaps the most well-known images of this period are from the memorable video of "Hurt," Johnny Cash's cover version of the song by Trent Reznor's Nine Inch Nails, on *The Man Comes Around.* Some have seen this short film as his epitaph, but that seems too easy. His last acts—not on film—were his epitaph. John was ill before June died, and quickly became sicker. So many previous chroniclers have said—and in this, they're not wrong—that it was altogether fitting and even poetic that June and John chased one another to heaven. In July of 2003, two months before his death, John performed one last time, at the Carter Family Fold, near Bristol, Tennessee, saying before he sang, "The spirit of June Carter overshadows me tonight with the love she had for me and the love I have for her. We connect somewhere between here and heaven. She came down for a short visit, I guess, from heaven to visit with me tonight to give me courage and inspiration like she always has."

It has been 15 years now that we've been without them, John and June. Their family was graced by their presence in this temporal realm, to be sure, and so were we, all of the fans of John and June and Vivian and Rosanne and John Carter and Maybelle and Tommy and Roy and Ray and Jack and Tara and . . . well, we needn't go on; the point is made: all of the fans of all of the Cashes and Carters—this remarkable American family that has reached out through the many years and touched us all.

ANDY EARL

In Nashville, 1996.

ANDY EARL

Printed in Great Britain
by Amazon

46027483R00057